SELECTED POEMS

PHILIPPE JACCOTTET

Selected and translated with an introduction by
Derek Mahon

Viking

VIKING

Penguin Books Ltd, Harmondsworth, Middlesex, England
Viking Penguin Inc., 40 West 23rd Street, New York, New York 10010, U.S.A.
Penguin Books Australia Ltd, Ringwood, Victoria, Australia
Penguin Books Canada Ltd, 2801 John Street, Markham, Ontario, Canada L3R 1B4
Penguin Books (N.Z.) Ltd, 182–190 Wairau Road, Auckland 10, New Zealand

First published 1987
Published simultaneously by Penguin Books
Poems copyright © Philippe Jaccottet, 1953, 1957, 1967, 1969, 1974, 1977, 1983
Selection, translation and introduction copyright © Derek Mahon, 1987

Typeset in Bembo

Printed in Great Britain by
Richard Clay Ltd, Bungay, Suffolk

British Library Cataloguing in Publication Data

Jaccottet, Philippe
    Selected poems.
    I. Title   II. Mahon, Derek
    841'.914   PQ2670.A225

    ISBN 0–670–81116–5

Contents

Introduction

Most readers approach contemporary French verse with trepidation, suspecting (often rightly) that what they are being asked to read will prove to be puzzling, gratuitous, angular, abstract, inflated and doctrinaire, bearing little resemblance to poetry as it is understood in the rest of the world. (We have fewer difficulties with Montale or Brodsky than with, say, Michaux or Deguy – who remain, for that reason, no more than names to most of us.) At the risk of making him seem more immediately graspable than he is, I think it's safe to say that prospective readers of Jaccottet need have no such fears. Unlike the closely interlocked cycles of his better known contemporary Yves Bonnefoy, which are hermetic and work according to a system, or the open-plan notations of André du Bouchet, Jaccottet's poems are recognizably circumstantial, and empirical in their relation to the 'real world'.

Although not quite so straightforward as Simon Watson Taylor's phrase, 'an artlessly artful simplicity', might suggest, he is really quite accessible to the anglophone reader. Unlike many French poets, he is not greatly troubled by the disjunction between the signifying word and the thing signified. Language is a given, and suffices for his purposes – which may explain his acceptance in the English-speaking world, where so much recent French poetry ('*la poésie illisible*': 'unreadable poetry', as it's called) has been greeted with baffled incomprehension. There is even, I think (though he himself might be startled by the idea), something 'English' in his mode of perception, something about him of a latter-day Keats – whose '*Ode à l'automne*' he quotes more than once in his prose works, and whose 'negative capability' he shares (a Geneva Protestant in origin, he is also not quite French in sensibility). To come closer to our own time, the sort of note he strikes is not unlike that of David Gascoyne's *Poems 1938–42*, works of mystical attention like 'A Wartime Dawn' and 'The Gravel-Pit Field' – or, at a later date, of Kathleen Raine's *On a Deserted Shore*, for which he has expressed admiration. Significantly, he has attracted the interest of a number of English-language poets; though his direct *influence* is nowhere clearly discernible, except perhaps in W. S. Merwin's *The Lice* (1969), where several pieces strike the Jaccottet note exactly. Take 'The Room':

> I think all this is somewhere in myself
> The cold room unlit before dawn
> Containing a stillness such as attends death
> And from a corner the sounds of a small bird trying
> From time to time to fly a few beats in the dark
> You would say it was dying it is immortal.

7

But I don't wish to create the impression that he is some kind of Anglo-American poet who writes in French; for, as Taylor points out, his effects 'are bound up with the nature, and indeed the structure, of the French language'. His Paris years coincided with the post-war Existentialist vogue and the final demise of Surrealism; but few French poets of the past fifty years have entirely escaped the Surrealist influence, and Jaccottet is no exception. Asked which French poet of recent times would be most likely to last, he named Éluard – the one indubitably fine poet the movement produced. Although closer to the lyrical phenomenology of Ponge, Jaccottet recognized Éluard's genius and shares, indeed, a measure of common ground. '*Il y a une autre réalité,*' Éluard had said, '*mais elle est en celle-ci*' ('There is another reality, but it resides in this one'); and this seeming paradox provides a key to Jaccottet's own work: he echoes Éluard with the phrase, '*l'autre monde présent peut-être dans celui-ci*' ('the other world present perhaps in this one'), and of a walk in wild country he observes, '*On dirait qu'on a changé de monde sans quitter celui-ci*' ('You would say you had changed worlds without leaving this one').★

He began as an urban poet, a poet of post-war Paris; *L'Effraie* ('The Screech Owl', 1953) – its title reminiscent of Baudelaire's owls, meditative sages compared with Jaccottet's ominous apparition – is full of alienation, existential fear and the onus of self-definition. The first poem in the volume, and therefore in the collected works, speaks already of death and the extinction of stars:

> already
> bone pierces the living skin
> while stars fade at the end of the street.

Within a few pages he has described himself as 'a stranger in this life' and declared that he 'possesses nothing'. There are love poems too; but it's not until *L'Ignorant* ('Ignorance', 1957), completed after his marriage and removal to Grignan, Drôme, that he starts to come into his own; and for many readers this remains his outstanding collection. Several of his most admired poems are there – the title poem, 'Patience', 'The Voice' and 'The Tenant'; but *L'Ignorant*, impressive though it is, was also a clearing of space for something else. Having declared himself an 'ignorant' man, without possessions, he was ready to make his most significant advance.

The title *Airs* (1967), which means both tunes and breezes, is best left as 'Airs' in English, since that way we retain the double meaning

---

★ Except where otherwise indicated, my prose quotations are taken from his poetic diary *La Semaison*, defined by Littré as '*la dispersion naturelle des graines d'une plante*': 'the natural dispersion of plant seeds'.

– an important consideration in the light of Jaccottet's reflections on 'breath': '*L'illimité est le souffle qui nous anime . . . La poésie est la parole que ce souffle alimente et porte, d'où son pouvoir sur nous*' ('The limitless is the breath which gives us life . . . Poetry is the word which this breath sustains and carries, whence its power over us'). The idea, familiar to us since the Romantics, goes back to the Book of Genesis. *Airs*, too, is concerned with beginnings: '*À partir de rien, là est ma loi. Tout le reste: fumée lointaine*' ('To start from nothing, that's my rule. Everything else: distant smoke'). There is something of Beckett about this, the Beckett who spoke, in the *Dialogues*, of 'an art unresentful of its insuperable indigence' and declared that 'to be an artist is to fail as no other dare fail: failure is his world and the shrink from it desertion'; but Jaccottet means to *start* from nothing, not to *end* there. He too speaks of '*le presque rien à dire*' ('the almost nothing to say'); but he finds Beckett too 'systematic' and, besides, Jaccottet is in love with the earth. Between flowery Grignan and Beckett's 'hole in the Marne mud' stretches a world of difference.

Grignan, says Michelin, is 'a small town on a rocky eminence between two valleys'. Mme de Sévigné is buried there. Some forty kilometres south of Grenoble, its situation and climate Alpine, it seems ideal for someone of Jaccottet's reclusive temperament. John Ardagh, in his chapter on the arts in *France in the 1980s* (Penguin Books, 1982), observes that 'only the most bold or brilliant spirit will dare to ignore or defy current fashions. If you cease to be seen and heard, if you go to live and work quietly in the provinces, then (unless your talent is exceptional) you cease to exist.' Jaccottet, though seldom seen or heard, has not 'ceased to exist', nor is his talent merely 'exceptional': it is of a very high order indeed. 'Outside the cliques, unbothered with the fashion', in MacNeice's phrase, he has pursued a private vision consciously resistant to systematization. So much has been written as the demonstration of a theory, or in anticipation of a certain kind of critical exposition, rather than as primary artistic endeavour, that Jaccottet's resistance to the trend (as to all formal philosophy – contrast Bonnefoy's interest in Hegel) has acquired an exemplary, even a heroic quality.

Given the critical context of recent years, it comes as no surprise to find Jean Starobinski, in his slightly orotund preface to Jaccottet's *Poésie 1946 – 1967*, beginning with an expression of surprise: 'We are seized with wonder and gratitude: are, then, poetic diction, poetic discourse . . . still possible?' And, thinking of deconstructionism, he points out that Jaccottet 'resists the tendency, nowadays widespread, to expel the author from the text, and to make of writing a reflexive activity which finds its energy only in itself. Jaccottet doesn't obliterate his identity; he stands by his word.' Note, though, that 'his work grows increasingly self-effacing and reticent; autobiographical detail gradually disappears'. Like other minimalists he knows exiguity and exasperation:

his *'Que reste-t-il?'* ('What remains?') places him in the tradition of
solitary inquiry of which Diogenes, Montaigne and *L'Innommable* are but
three examples: 'What remains to me is practically nothing; but it's like
a narrow gate you have to go through. The trick is to get through the
gate and make sure it doesn't close again completely'; and in *Éléments
d'un songe* he proclaims his purpose as *'tirer de la limite même un chant'*
('to draw a song from the very limit').

'An evident paradox', says Starobinski, 'associates, in this
work, ignorance with truth, makes of ignorance the receptacle of the
greatest truth, on condition that ignorance remains perpetually alert,
sensitive to . . . the contingencies of the world.' We've met that before,
of course. This Taoist conception of 'ignorance' owes something to
Keats's theory of negative capability. In the letter to Richard
Woodhouse dated 18 October 1818, Keats declared that 'the poetical
character is not itself – it has no self – it is everything and nothing – it
has no character'. It might be worth recalling here that Jaccottet is the
French translator of Musil's *The Man Without Qualities*, sometimes said
to be about 'the death of Europe' (*'à partir de rien'*?); but Musil's
protagonist, according to his English translators Eithne Wilkins and Ernst
Kaiser, 'has *given up* his qualities, *as an ascetic might give up the world*'
(my italics). The same is at least partly true of the 'ignorant' Jaccottet:

> I sit in my room and am silent. Silence
> arrives like a servant to tidy things up
> while I wait for the lies to disperse.

Besides Musil, Jaccottet has translated (and written a book about) Rilke,
a poet who died, when Jaccottet was four, not far from where Jaccottet
spent his childhood, and whose presence is often felt in his work. Like
Rilke, he wishes to be *'attentif à ce qui, d'un autre monde, affleure dans le
nôtre'* ('attentive to what, from another world, appears in our own') –
the classic definition of a miracle. And he asks himself the Rilkean,
which is to say the eternal, questions, sometimes providing quasi-Rilkean
answers. Behind Jaccottet lie lines from the *Duino Elegies* like 'the
uninterrupted news that grows out of silence' and '*Here* is the time of
the tellable, *here* is its home' (trans. J. B. Leishman) – though, in fairness
to Jaccottet, he shuns *'la tentation de s'isoler en oraison, ce qui gêne quelquefois
chez Rilke'* ('the temptation to lose oneself in prayer, so irritating at
times in Rilke'); and he writes 'for the air', not 'for the angel in the
church of the Laodiceans'.

But the Rilkean questions I have in mind are most clearly
formulated in *The Notebook of Malte Laurids Brigge*, written before the
death of Europe's *grande illusion* of itself, when 'we used to be rich'
(*Tenth Elegy*). Already Rilke perceives the world in a new way:

> I am learning to see. I don't know why, but
> everything penetrates more deeply within me and no longer stops
> where, until now, it always used to finish. I possess an inner self of

which I was ignorant . . . Here I sit in my little room, I, Brigge
. . . I sit here and am nothing. And nevertheless this nothing begins
to think and, five flights up, on a grey Parisian afternoon, thinks
. . . is it possible that nothing real or important has yet been seen
or known or said? Is it possible that despite our culture, religion
and worldly wisdom, we still remain on the surface of life? *Is it
possible that the whole history of the world has been misunderstood?* Yes,
it is possible . . . But if all this is possible then surely . . . something
must be done. *The first comer*, he who has had these disturbing
thoughts, must begin to do some of the neglected things.
(Trans. John Linton; my italics)

Jaccottet's work carries extra-poetical significance in as much
as it proposes, though without recounting, except in flashes of insight,
an alternative history of the world:

the grandeur of these too-predictable waters
leaves me cold since I no longer know
how to communicate. Let the 'fine days' go!

It is in this sense revolutionary, like the entry in Braque's notebook, *Le
Jour et la nuit*: '*Le présent, le fortuit, va nous libérer*' ('The present, the
fortuitous, will liberate us'). Sartre, of all people, specifically exempted
poetry from a direct concern with history (an exemption as patronizing
as it was well-intentioned); but, in his role of 'first comer', early riser,
Jaccottet attends to 'the neglected things':

At the end of the shadiest paths,
among brambles, you will find an anemone
bright and ordinary like the morning star.

Starobinski again:

To be an ignorant man, to possess nothing but a
fragile word, to find oneself as if relying upon darkness and
nothingness: that is the position from which one must be constantly
setting out. Setting out, starting again: Jaccottet doesn't resign
himself to immobility, he doesn't submit to failure. If 'the real
place' is inaccessible, the other mistake is to insist on living in the
dark, on burying oneself there in despair. When he writes, 'To start
from nothing, that's my rule', we recognize a necessary premise –
nothingness – but also an indication of departure. Departure on the
roads of the earth, without hope of conquest, with no certain goal.
But the word to which this gives rise, born of darkness and
nothingness, carries within it the possibility of a journey into light.
What light? Not that of the beyond, but that of each earthly dawn
. . . Jaccottet is one of the great poets of daybreak.

He is a secular mystic, an explorer of '*le vrai lieu*' ('the real
place'). 'The natural object is always the adequate symbol', said Pound;
and Jaccottet's symbols are the elemental, pre-Socratic ones: tree,
flower, sun, moon, road, mountain, wind, water, bird, house, lamp. He

is fascinated by light, especially what John le Carré calls 'the religious
light between dawn and morning'; and by lamplit twilight, *l'heure bleue*.
His characteristic posture is that of a man alone in a garden watching
the sun rise, *'rebaptisé chaque matin par le jour'* ('rebaptized each morning
by daybreak'), or seated at his desk at dusk *à la clarté déserte de sa lampe*.
'I wonder', mused Geoffrey Grigson in *Notes from an Odd Country*, 'if
deity and art don't originate in sparkle, glitter, crystal, refracted light,
an abstracted portion of sun. Hopkins staring at the shine in the gravel
after rain. *Paradise Lost*, Hölderlin, Ronsard . . . The dancing places
which shine, in Hesiod. "Immortal diamond".' *La Semaison* records
frequent light-readings:

> Ice, limpidity, sun. A few clouds clinging to the mountains.
> (January 1959)

> Violent mistral: the Mont Ventoux hidden by a grey-pink mist.
> (April 1959)

> Mauve, lilac clouds. Paper nearly blue. A dying fire.
> I can hardly see the words now. (October 1959)

> Be faithful to immediate experience. (November 1959)

Jaccottet is an intensely visual poet, and this brings us to the
question of art; for French poets are formed by artistic as well as poetic
tradition. At least since Baudelaire there has existed in France a peculiarly
intimate relation between poet and painter, between poet and printer
even. A book of verse, especially the limited edition, is conceived as a
total work of art: the paper, the ink, the binding contribute as much as
the text and, where they occur, the illustrations. (The phenomenon is
universal now: various English, Irish and American publishers have
adopted the *livre d'art*.) The relevance of this to Jaccottet is not
immediately obvious, but swiftly becomes so if his work is considered
in certain lights. His wife is an artist, specializing in landscape and still
life; and she has illustrated his work. So too, by anticipation, have
Cézanne and (I suggest) Bonnard. What the Mont Ste Victoire was to
Cézanne, the Mont Ventoux is to Jaccottet. He lives in its shadow,
makes frequent allusion to it in *La Semaison*; and its presence is felt in
his poems from *L'Ignorant* to *Pensées sous les nuages*. Michelin again:

> VENTOUX, Mont, *Vaucluse*. Some of the most astonishing views of
> Provence, either from the flanks of the massif or from the summit
> (over 1900 m), from which can be seen the Alps, the Vercors, the
> Cévennes, Ste Victoire, Marseille, the sea, and at night the flashing
> of lighthouses. The atmosphere tends to be hazy at midday in hot
> weather. Meteorological observatory, radar and television
> installations. Snow from December to April: skiing from Chalet
> Renard and Mont Serein. Remarkable flora.

Bonnard is a guess. There is a *figurative* analogy, a disregard
in each for formal experiment in the analytic sense; there is a similar

intimisme in their treatment of domestic interiors, open windows and gardens; both are colourists; and for both

> This world is merely the tip
> of an unseen conflagration.

Consider Bonnard's *Snow Garden* (1900), where the dusk is inflamed by a red blaze from the setting sun. Garden, snow and light combine in a fierce synthesis such as Jaccottet himself often achieves. Jean Grenier, in *La Galerie des Arts* (no. 41, February 1967), says of Bonnard that 'he had a child-like vision which transforms the quotidian into the marvellous. The scene needn't be unusual or impressive: on the contrary, it's the most familiar things which exercise the strongest hold upon his attention.' Nabokov, in *The Real Life of Sebastian Knight*, says of Clare Bishop that 'she possessed that real sense of beauty which has less to do with art than with the constant readiness to discern the halo round a frying-pan or the likeness between a weeping-willow and a Skye terrier'. They might have been speaking of Jaccottet.

But the artist with whom he has the greatest affinity is Pierre Tal-Coat, who contributed engravings to the first (limited) edition of Jaccottet's *À travers un verger* (1982). Breton in origin, he was born in 1905, spent many years in Paris, and withdrew in 1945 to Aix-en-Provence, which makes him a not-too-distant neighbour of the poet. Tal-Coat's characteristic manner, as developed in the 1950s, has been called 'lyrical abstraction': a natural scene or object is teased out until precise subject-matter disappears. A cosmic mysticism was ascribed to such Tal-Coat series as *Terres* (1966) and *Herbes* (1967); and the influence of Chinese landscape-painting has been noted. Pictures like *Paysage d'Aix* (1950), *Pluie sur la Ste Victoire* (1952) and the ink drawing *Plateau cévenol* (1954) are relevant here, particularly the last, a few brush-strokes only, black on white, which qualifies, so to speak, as an ideogram, even as a haiku (what Grigson called 'a few words in space'); and here is the connection with Jaccottet, for he too developed a mode of lyrical abstraction based, very consciously, on oriental precedents. *Airs* is a book of very short poems which, says the author, '*raconte de façon cachée une histoire d'amour*' ('contains a hidden love story' – letter to the translator. No more than a quarter of the full sequence appears in the present selection.) The love story is there, certainly, but the most striking thing about the poems is their technique: a few brush-strokes only, a few words in space, in startling contrast to the fairly traditional rhetoric of *L'Effraie* and *L'Ignorant*; and, few as the lines are, we have to read between them.

What do we miss in this poetry? Several things: vitality sometimes, humour, the demotic, the abrasive surfaces of the modern world. It's sparsely populated, and there's a certain thinness of texture, albeit deliberate. Sometimes it seems refined out of existence. There is (almost) no *sea*: this is an inland poetry of river and mountain, the

country road, the lake in the woods. People? He is married, with two
children, a son and a daughter; and, besides the more explicit love
poems, one often makes out the comforting, Muse-like presence of his
wife; but, except for actual brief appearances, as in 'Glimpses' (in *Pensées
sous les nuages*), she remains a shadowy figure. '*Impossible*', notes
Jaccottet, '*de parler d'êtres proches tant qu'ils sont vivants et proches, à moins
d'une impudeur dont je ne suis pas capable*' ('Impossible to speak of my nearest
and dearest while they are alive beside me, an indecency of which I am
incapable'). One recognizably human figure is his father-in-law, the
dying man of *Leçons* ('Lessons', 1969): here we know ourselves in the
presence of a vigorous old boy astounded by his own approaching death:

> He who had always loved his garden, his walls,
> who had kept the keys of the house.

A human drama, an interior *voyage au bout de la nuit*, is enacted before
our eyes in this volume, and at times the pain is almost unbearable. Raw
emotion reduces many of the poems to shocked annotation: '*De plus en
plus j'entends le mensonge des paroles, ce qui me paralyse*' ('Increasingly I
hear the *lying* of words, which paralyses me'). And he continues: 'What
makes expression hard for me now is that I don't want to cheat – and
it seems to me that most cheat, more or less, with their own experience;
put it between parentheses, make it vanish.'

Chants d'en bas ('Songs from Below', 1974), like *Leçons*
described as a *livre de deuil*, 'a mourning book', expresses something of
this in verse:

> To speak is to lie, or worse: a craven
> insult to grief or a waste
> of the little time and energy at our disposal.

This poetic self-suspicion appears again in *À la lumière d'hiver* ('Winter
Light', 1977), where Jaccottet seems to review, in a slightly sardonic
fashion, his achievement to date – by most standards, considerable; by
his own, nugatory. Yet he implicitly concedes value – perhaps,
paradoxically, the greatest value – to the art of which he represents
himself as a 'self-effacing' practitioner:

> (Nothing at all, a footfall on the road,
> yet more mysterious than guide or god.)

In some ways an old-fashioned, 'timeless' poet, capable of a
phrase like '*bergers naïfs*' ('simple shepherds'), he has spoken of '*la goutte
d'eau pur*' ('the pure water-drop') of poetry, contrasting it with the
Byzantine theoretical complexity favoured by the mad scientists of
deconstruction: 'Such nonsense to set up against so much knowledge,
ingenuity, doctrine! No argument, certainly; but perhaps poetry relies
precisely on what is not argument. I, at least, rely on it.' The 'pure
water-drop', visible in *Airs*, grows audible in the magnificent *Pensées sous
les nuages* ('Cloud Thoughts', 1983), a volume which moves from the
photographic mode of 'Glimpses' to the celebratory music of 'To Henry

Purcell', a sequence written after hearing James Bowman perform in the Paris church of St Julien-le-Pauvre. (The poems I've chosen from *Chants d'en bas*, *À la lumière d'hiver* and *Pensées sous les nuages* are excerpted in each case from much longer *sequences*, which considerations of space prevented me from including in their entirety.)

We've spoken of art, and now we must speak of music, which is where, for the present, Jaccottet leaves off. *La Semaison* records his 'dream of writing a poem as fresh and alive as a piece of music, *pure but not cold*. Regret at not being a musician, at not having their skill or their freedom [my italics].' Of admired music like Verdi's *Requiem* or Mahler's *Lied von der Erde* he remarks: '*On est à peine capable de quelques mots en marge*' ('One is barely capable of a few words in the margin'). 'To Henry Purcell' consists of just such 'a few words':

> What do we hear
> who tune in to the night?
> A leisurely snow
> of crystal.

Dryden, writing of Purcell's *Songs and Airs*, observed that 'music and poetry have long been acknowledged sisters. Both of them may excel apart, but sure they are most excellent when they are joined, because nothing is then wanting to either of their perfections'; and it may be that one should listen to a recording of Purcell as an accompaniment to Jaccottet's homage. Yet, 'in the greatest art', suggests Susan Sontag in her essay 'On Style', 'one is always aware of things that cannot be said; of the contradiction between expression and the presence of the inexpressible. Stylistic devices are also techniques of avoidance. The most potent elements in a work of art are, often, its silences'; and Jaccottet's poems take place, characteristically, in the absence of other noise. Existential lyrics, minimalist and disabused, they leave, in Beckett's phrase, 'a stain upon the silence'. But to the tentative birdsong, running water and rustling leaves of the Jaccottet landscape one might add an intellectual music, what Dryden would have called the music of the spheres:

> If ever they speak above us
> in the starry trees of their April.

René Char, of whom Jaccottet has written appreciatively, called poetry '*la vie future à l'intérieur de l'homme requalifié*' ('the future interior life of requalified man'). Coleridge argued that 'the great instrument of moral good is the imagination, and poetry administers to the effect by acting upon the cause'; and Rilke, says Jaccottet, set himself the greatest task of all: '*le salut du monde, une chance de vie pour l'homme*' ('the salvation of the world, a chance of life for mankind'). These are large claims, but Jaccottet measures up to them. In his exemplary dedication, in the excellence of his art, and in his anticipation of '*la vie future*', he will, I believe, come to be recognized as one of the finest

European poets of the century. Born in Switzerland, a translator of *Death in Venice*, he would be familiar with the 'Snow' chapter in *The Magic Mountain* where, in Mann's words, Hans Castorp 'dreams his dream of love'. One passage, a famous one, seems to me to encapsulate much of the matter in hand:

> I will keep faith with death in my heart, yet remember that faith with death is hostile to humankind as soon as we give it power over thought and action. *For the sake of goodness and love, man shall let death have no sovereignty over his thoughts.* And with this I awake; for I have dreamed it out to the end, I have come to my goal . . . Deep into the snow mountains my search has led me; now I have it fast. My dream has given it me, in utter clearness, that I may know it for ever . . . Open your eyes. Look: fair weather!
> (Trans. H. T. Lowe-Porter; Mann's italics)

A translator himself, Jaccottet has been indulgent towards my inadequate versions of his work. I have tried, in his own words, to be 'attentive to a foreign voice, and to give to this voice, with the resources of our own language, an embodiment in which the original inflection survives'; but I don't deceive myself in this respect: translation is only translation . . . My thanks to Philippe Jaccottet for his patience and encouragement; Paul Keegan for his support; Stephen and Bridget Romer for their practical assistance; Professor Roger Little and Jean-Paul Pittion of Dublin University for their advice; and Geraldine Mangan for her secretarial help. What Alastair Reid calls 'the translation police' may, however, take it from me that all errors and ineptitudes are my own.

Select Bibliography

Books by Philippe Jaccottet

Requiem, Mermod, 1947.
L'Effraie, Gallimard, 1953.
La Promenade sous les arbres (prose), Mermod, 1957.
L'Ignorant, Gallimard, 1957.
Éléments d'un songe (prose), Gallimard, 1961.
L'Obscurité (prose), Gallimard, 1961.
La Semaison (prose), Payot, 1963; Gallimard, 1971 and 1984.
Airs, Gallimard, 1967.
L'Entretien des Muses (prose), Gallimard, 1968.
Leçons, Payot, 1969.
Paysages avec figures absentes (prose), Gallimard, 1970.
Rilke (prose), Seuil (Écrivains de Toujours), 1970.
Poésie 1946–1967, Gallimard, 1971.
Chants d'en bas, Payot, 1974.
À la lumière d'hiver, Gallimard, 1977.
Pensées sous les nuages, Gallimard, 1983.
À travers un verger (prose), Gallimard, 1984.
Une Transaction secrète (prose), Gallimard, 1987.

About Philippe Jaccottet

There is a considerable literature about Jaccottet, much of it in periodical form; but the best general introduction is Alain Clerval's *Philippe Jaccottet*, Seghers (Poètes d'Aujourd'hui), 1976. Previous translators of individual poems or groups of poems include Cid Corman, Michael Hamburger, Donald Justice, W. S. Merwin, John Montague, David Pryce-Jones, Anthony Rudolf, Peter Scupham, Simon Watson Taylor and Charles Tomlinson, all of whose efforts proved helpful at different points.

Acknowledgement is made to the editors of *The Times Literary Supplement*, the *Observer*, the *Spectator*, *Agenda*, *Verse*, *Poetry Ireland*, *Hermathena* and the *Irish Times*, where some of these translations first appeared.

from L'Effraie (1953)

from The Screech Owl (1953)

La nuit est une grande cité endormie
où le vent souffle . . . Il est venu de loin jusqu'à
l'asile de ce lit. C'est la minuit de juin.
Tu dors, on m'a mené sur ces bords infinis,
le vent secoue le noisetier. Vient cet appel
qui se rapproche et se retire, on jurerait
une lueur fuyant à travers bois, ou bien
les ombres qui tournoient, dit-on, dans les enfers.
(Cet appel dans la nuit d'été, combien de choses
j'en pourrais dire, et de tes yeux . . .) Mais ce n'est que
l'oiseau nommé l'effraie, qui nous appelle au fond
de ces bois de banlieue. Et déjà notre odeur
est celle de la pourriture au petit jour,
déjà sous notre peau si chaude perce l'os,
tandis que sombrent les étoiles au coin des rues.

The June night is like a city of the dead
where the wind sighs, wind that has come
a long way to the shelter of our bed.
It shakes a hazel while you sleep
and I drift to the edge of a dream;
then I hear cries, nearby, far-off,
like fugitive lights in a forest
or shadows flickering in hell.
(So much to be said of those cries
and so much to be said of your eyes!)
It's only a bird, the screech owl,
in the thick of these urban woods;
but already our smell is the smell
of something rotten at dawn; already
bone pierces the living skin
while stars fade at the end of the street.

Comme je suis un étranger dans notre vie,
je ne parle qu'à toi avec d'étranges mots,
parce que tu seras peut-être ma patrie,
mon printemps, nid de paille et de pluie aux rameaux,

ma ruche d'eau qui tremble à la pointe du jour,
ma naissante Douceur-dans-la-nuit . . . (Mais c'est l'heure
que les corps heureux s'enfouissent dans leur amour
avec des cris de joie, et une fille pleure

dans la cour froide. Et toi? Tu n'es pas dans la ville,
tu ne marches pas à la rencontre des nuits,
c'est l'heure où seul avec ces paroles faciles

je me souviens d'une bouche réelle . . .) Ô fruits
mûrs, source des chemins dorés, jardins de lierre,
je ne parle qu'à toi, mon absente, ma terre . . .

Being a stranger in this life, I speak
only to you, and in strange sentences,
since you may prove the familiar land I seek,
my spring, my dewy straw-nest in the branches,

my gush of water trembling at first light,
my budding Sweetness-in-the-Dark; but now
while striving bodies dive to their delight
with cries of love, a lone girl whimpers low

in the cold yard. And you? You're out of reach,
not marching out tonight to face the town.
Lying alone here with my facile speech

I think of your real mouth . . . O ripening fruits
and ivied gardens, depths of golden lane,
I speak only to you, my absent roots.

Je sais maintenant que je ne possède rien,
pas même ce bel or qui est feuilles pourries,
encore moins ces jours volant d'hier à demain
à grands coups d'ailes vers une heureuse patrie.

Elle fut avec eux, l'émigrante fanée,
la beauté faible, avec ses secrets décevants,
vêtue de brume. On l'aura sans doute emmenée
ailleurs, par ces forêts pluvieuses. Comme avant,

je me retrouve au seuil d'un hiver irréel
où chante le bouvreuil obstiné, seul appel
qui ne cesse pas, comme le lierre. Mais qui peut dire

quel est son sens? Je vois ma santé se réduire,
pareille à ce feu bref au-devant du brouillard
qu'un vent glacial avive, efface . . . Il se fait tard.

I know now I possess nothing of my own –
not even the gold of these dead leaves, still less
these days flying past into the unknown
beating their great wings toward what happy place.

The exhausted emigrant, she was there too,
a frail beauty with her mysterious lore
mist-clothed. No doubt they've taken her by now
elsewhere in these dripping forests. As before

I stand on the threshold of a wintry sky
listening to one fierce finch, its deathless cry
as obstinate as ivy. Who can translate

its meaning? Now my strength begins to fail
like the brief fire in the fog an icy gale
fans and extinguishes. It's getting late.

Portovenere

La mer est de nouveau obscure. Tu comprends,
c'est la dernière nuit. Mais qui vais-je appelant?
Hors l'écho, je ne parle à personne, à personne.
Où s'écroulent les rocs, la mer est noire, et tonne
dans sa cloche de pluie. Une chauve-souris
cogne aux barreaux de l'air d'un vol comme surpris,
tous ces jours sont perdus, déchirés par ses ailes
noires, la majesté de ces eaux trop fidèles
me laisse froid, puisque je ne parle toujours
ni à toi, ni à rien. Qu'ils sombrent, ces 'beaux jours' !
Je pars, je continue à vieillir, peu m'importe,
sur qui s'en va la mer saura claquer la porte.

Portovenere

The sea is dark again on my last night
but who or what am I calling upon tonight?
Aside from the echo there is nobody, nobody.
Beyond the crumbling rocks the iron-dark sea
booms in its bell of rain, and a bat flies
at the windows of the air in wild surprise.
My days, torn by its black wings, are in tatters;
the grandeur of these too-predictable waters
leaves me cold since I no longer know
how to communicate. Let the 'fine days' go!
I leave, an older man, what do I care,
the sea will slam its door on my departure.

Intérieur

Il y a longtemps que je cherche à vivre ici,
dans cette chambre que je fais semblant d'aimer,
la table, les objets sans soucis, la fenêtre
ouvrant au bout de chaque nuit d'autres verdures,
et le coeur du merle bat dans le lierre sombre,
partout des lueurs achèvent l'ombre vieillie.

J'accepte moi aussi de croire qu'il fait doux,
que je suis chez moi, que la journée sera bonne.
Il y a juste, au pied du lit, cette araignée
(à cause du jardin), je ne l'ai pas assez
piétinée, on dirait qu'elle travaille encore
au piège qui attend mon fragile fantôme . . .

Interior

I have been trying for a long time to live
here in this room I pretend to like
with its table, its thoughtless objects,
its window wide to the dawn leaves.
A blackbird throbs in the ivy; light
everywhere polishes off the ancient dark.

I would gladly believe the bad times are done,
that this is my home, that the sun will shine,
were it not for the spider in the dust
at the foot of the bed, strayed in from the garden.
I should have trampled it harder, you would think
it was still weaving a trap for my delicate ghost.

Les eaux et les forêts

I   La clarté de ces bois en mars est irréelle,
tout est encor si frais qu'à peine insiste-t-elle.
Les oiseaux ne sont pas nombreux; tout juste si,
très loin, où l'aubépine éclaire les taillis,
le coucou chante. On voit scintiller des fumées
qui emportent ce qu'on brûla d'une journée,
la feuille morte sert les vivantes couronnes,
et suivant la leçon des plus mauvais chemins,
sous les ronces, on rejoint le nid de l'anémone,
claire et commune comme l'étoile du matin.

II   Quand même je saurais le réseau de mes nerfs
aussi précaire que le toile d'araignée,
je n'en louerais pas moins ces merveilles de vert,
ces colonnes, même choisies pour la cognée,

et ces chevaux de bûcherons . . . Ma confiance
devrait s'étendre un jour à la hache, à l'éclair,
si la beauté de mars n'est que l'obéissance
du merle et de la violette, par temps clair.

III   Le dimanche peuple les bois d'enfants qui geignent,
de femmes vieillissantes; un garçon sur deux saigne
au genou, et l'on rentre avec des mouchoirs gris,
laissant de vieux papiers près de l'étang . . . Les cris
s'éloignent avec la lumière. Sous les charmes,
une fille tire sur sa jupe à chaque alarme,
l'air harassé. Toute douceur, celle de l'air
ou de l'amour, a la cruauté pour revers,
tout beau dimanche a sa rançon, comme les fêtes
ces taches sur les tables où le jour nous inquiète.

IV   Toute autre inquiétude est encore futile,
je ne marcherai pas longtemps dans ces forêts,
et la parole n'est ni plus ni moins utile
que ces chatons de saule en terrain de marais:

peu importe qu'ils tombent en poussière s'ils brillent,
bien d'autres marcheront dans ces bois qui mourront,
peu importe que la beauté tombe pourrie,
puisqu'elle semble en la totale soumission.

Streams and Forests

I   The brightness of these March woods is unreal,
everything still so fresh it hardly insists.
Not many birds yet; but where whitethorn
brightens the thickets a cuckoo sings,
and sparkling smoke carries away
whatever it was that was burnt today.
Dead leaves will make the living crown.
At the end of the shadiest paths,
among brambles, you will find an anemone
bright and ordinary like the morning star.

II   Even if I could examine the cobweb intricacies
of my nervous system, I would still
be able to praise these wooden
columns, even those chosen for destruction.

If the beauty of March consists in the obedience
of blackbird and violet to a clear sky,
I too must extend my confidence one day
to the lightning-flash of the axe.

III   Sunday fills the woods with complaining children,
ageing women, boys with bloody knees
and dirty handkerchiefs; and the pond
is littered with crumpled newspapers.
Shouts fade with the light. Under the elms
a girl tugs resentfully at her skirt
if anyone passes. All gentleness, of the air
or of love, is harsh on the other side:
fine Sundays have their price, like parties
that leave wine-stains on the table at daybreak.

IV   All this anxiety is beside the point,
my walking in these woods will not be long,
and words are neither more nor less useful
than the willows rustling in the marshes.

Dust-destined, yes; but the dust glitters:
other mortals will walk here when I've gone.
As for the death of beauty, that hardly matters:
it shines forth in its very abdication.

from L'Ignorant (1957)

from Ignorance (1957)

Au petit jour

I   La nuit n'est pas ce que l'on croit, revers du feu,
chute du jour et négation de la lumière,
mais subterfuge fait pour nous ouvrir les yeux
sur ce qui reste irrévélé tant qu'on l'éclaire.

Les zélés serviteurs du visible éloignés,
sous le feuillage des ténèbres est établie
le demeure de la violette, le dernier
refuge de celui qui vieillit sans patrie . . .

II   Comme l'huile qui dort dans la lampe et bientôt
tout entière se change en lueur et respire
sous la lune emportée par le vol des oiseaux,
tu murmures et tu brûles. (Mais comment dire
cette chose qui est trop pure pour la voix?)
Tu es le feu naissant sur les froides rivières,
l'alouette jaillie du champ . . . Je vois en toi
s'ouvrir et s'entêter la beauté de la terre.

III   Je te parle, mon petit jour. Mais tout cela
ne serait-il qu'un vol de paroles dans l'air?
Nomade est la lumière. Celle qu'on embrassa
devient celle qui fut embrassée, et se perd.
Qu'une dernière fois dans la voix qui l'implore
elle se lève donc et rayonne, l'aurore.

Daybreak

I   Night is not what we think, the reverse of fire,
sun–death and the negation of the light,
but a device to discover
whatever remains invisible in daylight.

The zealous servants of the visible
having withdrawn, the violet has made
its home now in the deepening shade,
the final refuge of the exiled soul.

II   Like the oil asleep in the lamp which suddenly,
beneath a moon swept by a flight of birds,
transforms itself to a glow and breathes,
you murmur and burn; and no human voice
can convey the quality of it.
You are the light rising on cold rivers,
the lark sprung from the field;
the very earth is laid bare and elated.

III   I speak to you, daybreak, although what I say
may weigh no more than a bird in flight.
Light is fugitive, embrace it
and it becomes a shade; but one
more time, as if it had heard me pray,
the sun rises and sends forth its first light.

La patience

Dans les cartes à jouer abattues sous la lampe
comme les papillons écroulés poussiéreux,
à travers le tapis de table et la fumée,
je vois ce qu'il vaut mieux ne voir pas affleurer
lorsque le tintement de l'heure dans les verres
annonce une nouvelle insomnie, la croissante
peur d'avoir peur dans le resserrement du temps,
l'usure du corps, l'éloignement des défenseurs.
Le vieil homme écarte les images passées
et, non sans réprimer un tremblement, regarde
la pluie glacée pousser la porte du jardin.

Patience

In the playing-cards spread out in the lamplight
like the powdery wings of fallen moths
I see beyond the smoke-wreathed tablecloths
something that would be better kept from sight –
a new insomnia the rung glasses chime,
fear of being afraid, contraction of time,
bodily attrition, collapse of resistance.
Old men discard their previous existence,
quelling a qualm, and turn to contemplate
the hailstones slashing at the garden gate.

La voix

Qui chante là quand toute voix se tait? Qui chante
avec cette voix sourde et pure un si beau chant?
Serait-ce hors de la ville, à Robinson, dans un
jardin couvert de neige? Ou est-ce là tout près,
quelqu'un qui ne se doutait pas qu'on l'écoutât?
Ne soyons pas impatients de le savoir
puisque le jour n'est pas autrement précédé
par l'invisible oiseau. Mais faisons seulement
silence. Une voix monte, et comme un vent de mars
aux bois vieillis porte leur force, elle nous vient
sans larmes, souriant plutôt devant la mort.
Qui chantait là quand notre lampe s'est éteinte?
Nul ne le sait. Mais seul peut entendre le coeur
qui ne cherche la possession ni la victoire.

The Voice

What is it that sings when the other voices are silent?
Whose is that pure, deaf voice, that sibilant song?
Is it down the road on a snow-covered lawn
or close at hand, unaware of an audience?
This is the mysterious first bird of dawn.
Do you hear the voice increase in volume
and, as a March wind quickens a creaking tree,
sing mildly to us without fear,
content in the fact of death? Do you hear?
What does it sing in the grey dawn? Nobody knows;
but the voice is audible only to those
whose hearts seek neither possession nor victory.

L'ignorant

Plus je vieillis et plus je croîs en ignorance,
plus j'ai vécu, moins je possède et moins je règne.
Tout ce que j'ai, c'est un espace tour à tour
enneigé ou brillant, mais jamais habité.
Où est le donateur, le guide, le gardien?
Je me tiens dans ma chambre et d'abord je me tais
(le silence entre en serviteur mettre un peu d'ordre),
et j'attends qu'un à un les mensonges s'écartent:
que reste-t-il? que reste-t-il à ce mourant
qui l'empêche si bien de mourir? Quelle force
le fait encor parler entre ses quatre murs?
Pourrais-je le savoir, moi l'ignare et l'inquiet?
Mais je l'entends vraiment qui parle, et sa parole
pénètre avec le jour, encore que bien vague:

'Comme le feu, l'amour n'établit sa clarté
que sur la faute et la beauté des bois en cendres . . .'

Ignorance

The older I grow the more ignorant I become,
the longer I live the less I possess or control.
All I have is a little space, snow-dark
or glittering, never inhabited.
Where is the giver, the guide, the guardian?
I sit in my room and am silent. Silence
arrives like a servant to tidy things up
while I wait for the lies to disperse.
And what remains to this dying man
that so well prevents him from dying?
What does he find to say to the four walls?
I hear him talking still, and his words
come in with the dawn, imperfectly understood:

'Love, like fire, can only reveal its brightness
on the failure and the beauty of burnt wood.'

Les gitans

Il y a un feu sous les arbres:
on l'entend qui parle bas
à la nation endormie
près des portes de la ville.

Si nous marchons en silence,
âmes de peu de durée
entre les sombres demeures,
c'est de crainte que tu meures,
murmure perpétuel
de la lumière cachée.

The Gipsies

There are fires under the trees:
you can hear the low voices of the tribe
encamped at the city gates.

If, short-lived souls that we are,
we pass silently
on the dark road tonight,
it is for fear you should die,
perpetual murmur
around the hidden light.

L'inattendu

Je ne fais pas grand-chose contre le démon:
je travaille, et levant les yeux parfois de mon
travail, je vois la lune avant qu'il fasse clair.

Que reste-t-il ainsi qui brille d'un hiver?
À la plus petite heure du matin je sors,
la neige emplit l'espace jusqu'aux plus fins bords,
l'herbe s'incline devant ce muet salut,
là se révèle ce que nul n'espérait plus.

The Unexpected

I don't pay much attention to the fiend.
I work and, looking up sometimes,
I see the moon before light dawns.

What is left shining of winter?
When I go out before daybreak
snow stretches to the farthest limits
and grass bows to its silent greeting,
revealing what one had no longer hoped for.

Sur les pas de la lune

M'étant penché en cette nuit à la fenêtre,
je vis que le monde était devenu léger
et qu'il n'y avait plus d'obstacles. Tout ce qui
nous retient dans le jour semblait plutôt devoir
me porter maintenant d'une ouverture à l'autre
à l'intérieur d'une demeure d'eau vers quelque chose
de très faible et de très lumineux comme l'herbe:
j'allais entrer dans l'herbe sans aucune peur,
j'allais rendre grâce à la fraîcheur de la terre,
sur les pas de la lune je dis oui et je m'en fus . . .

In the Steps of the Moon

Leaning out of the window tonight
I saw that the world was without weight
and there were no more obstacles. All
that detains us by day appeared, moreover,
to take me through one door after another
in an abode of water, towards something
as frail and luminous as the grass
I was about to enter without fear,
giving thanks for the freshness of the earth.
In the steps of the moon I said yes and off I went.

Paroles dans l'air

L'air si clair dit: 'Je fus un temps votre maison,
puis viendront d'autres voyageurs à votre place,
et vous qui aimiez tant ce séjour, où irez-
vous? Je vois bien de la poussière sur la terre,
mais vous me regardiez, et vos yeux paraissaient
ne pas m'être inconnus; mais vous chantiez parfois,
est-ce donc tout? Vous parliez même à demi-voix
à quelqu'un qui était souvent ensommeillé,
vous lui disiez que la lumière de la terre
était trop pure pour ne pas avoir un sens
qui échappât de quelque manière à la mort,
vous vous imaginiez avancer dans ce sens,
et cependant je ne vous entends plus: qu'avez-
vous fait? Que va penser surtout votre compagne?'

Elle répond à travers ses heureuses larmes:
'Il s'est changé en cette ombre qui lui plaisait.'

Words in the Air

The clear air said: 'I was your home once
but other guests have taken your place;
where will you go who liked it here so much?
You looked at me through the thick dust
of the earth, and your eyes were known to me.
You sang sometimes, you even whispered low
to someone else who was often asleep,
you told her the light of the earth
was too pure not to point a direction
which somehow avoided death. You imagined
yourself advancing in that direction;
but now I no longer hear you. What have you done?
Above all, what is your lover going to think?'

And she, his friend, replied through tears of happiness:
'He has changed into the shade that pleased him best.'

Le locataire

Nous habitons une maison légère haut dans les airs,
le vent et la lumière la cloisonnent en se croisant,
parfois tout est si clair que nous en oublions les ans,
nous volons dans un ciel à chaque porte plus ouvert.

Les arbres sont en bas, l'herbe plus bas, le monde vert,
scintillant le matin et, quand vient la nuit, s'éteignant,
et les montagnes qui respirent dans l'éloignement
sont si minces que le regard errant passe au travers.

La lumière est bâtie sur un abîme, elle est tremblante,
hâtons-nous donc de demeurer dans ce vibrant séjour,
car elle s'enténèbre de poussière en peu de jours
ou bien elle se brise et tout à coup nous ensanglante.

Porte le locataire dans la terre, toi, servante!
Il a les yeux fermés, nous l'avons trouvé dans la cour,
si tu lui as donné entre deux portes ton amour,
descends-le maintenant dans l'humide maison des plantes.

The Tenant

We live in an airy house in the cloud kingdom
with wind and sun instead of ceilings and floors.
Sometimes it is all so clear we forget the time
and fly in a heaven of ever more open doors.

There are trees down there, grass, a whole green world
glittering in the morning, extinguished at night;
as for the dozing mountains, fold upon fold,
the eye sees straight through them, they are so slight.

The light stands on a ravine and trembles there.
Be quick, then, to inhabit this vibrant hut,
for it will darken with dust in a month or a year
and cave in, covering us with blood and soot.

Bury the tenant in the earth, maidservant, lover:
his eyes are closed, we found him in the yard.
Having nursed him from the one door to the other,
now lay him out in his moist leguminous bed.

Que la fin nous illumine

Sombre ennemi qui nous combats et nous resserres,
laisse-moi, dans le peu de jours que je détiens,
vouer ma faiblesse et ma force à la lumière:
et que je sois changé en éclair à la fin.

Moins il y a d'avidité et de faconde
en nos propos, mieux on les néglige pour voir
jusque dans leur hésitation briller le monde
entre le matin ivre et la légèreté du soir.

Moins nos larmes apparaîtront brouillant nos yeux
et nos personnes par la crainte garrottées,
plus les regards iront s'éclaircissant et mieux
les égarés verront les portes enterrées.

L'effacement soit ma façon de resplendir,
la pauvreté surcharge de fruits notre table,
la mort, prochaine ou vague selon son désir,
soit l'aliment de la lumière inépuisable.

That the End Enlighten Us

Dark enemy, you who brace us in the fight,
let me, in the few days still left to spend,
devote my strength and weakness to the light
and so be changed to lightning in the end.

The gabbling mouths and animated eyes
grow easier to ignore even as they work:
the world gleams in their very hesitancies
between high morning and light-headed dark.

If we could stop whining and overcome
the fear that strangles us, behind, before,
our vision might improve, the lost become
more confident in their search for the buried door.

Let self-effacement be my way of blazing
and poverty weigh our table down with fruit;
death, far or near according to its choosing,
sustain, as ever, the inexhaustible light.

Dans un tourbillon de neige

Ils chevauchent encore dans les espaces glacés,
les quelques cavaliers que la mort n'a pas pu lasser.

Ils allument des feux dans la neige de loin en loin,
à chaque coup de vent il en flambe au moins un de moins.

Ils sont incroyablement petits, sombres, pressés,
devant l'immense, blanc et lent malheur à terrasser.

Certes, ils n'amassent plus dans leurs greniers ni or ni foin,
mais y cachant l'espoir fourbi avec le plus grand soin.

Ils courent les chemins par le pesant monstre effacés,
peut-être se font-ils si petits pour le mieux chasser?

Finalement, c'est bien toujours avec le même poing
qu'on se défend contre le souffle de l'immonde groin.

During a Snowstorm

I see them ride still in the icy places,
those few horsemen death never reduces.

They light fires here and there in the snow,
fires that go out whenever the winds blow.

Such tiny figures, desperate and dark
before the great white adversary they seek.

Their lofts, of course, hold neither gold nor grain,
merely the bright hope polished with such pain.

They pursue trails erased by the monster's size,
having grown small to take it by surprise.

In the end we always make use of the same fist
to fight off the bad breath of the foul beast.

Les distances

Tournent les martinets dans les hauteurs de l'air:
plus haut encore tournent les astres invisibles.
Que le jour se retire aux extrémités de la terre,
apparaîtront ces feux sur l'étendue de sombre sable . . .

Ainsi nous habitons un domaine de mouvements
et de distances; ainsi le coeur
va de l'arbre à l'oiseau, de l'oiseau aux astres lointains,
de l'astre à son amour. Ainsi l'amour
dans la maison fermée s'accroît, tourne et travaille,
serviteur des soucieux portant une lampe à la main.

Distances

Swifts turn in the heights of the air;
higher still turn the invisible stars.
When day withdraws to the ends of the earth
their fires shine on a dark expanse of sand.

We live in a world of motion and distance.
The heart flies from tree to bird,
from bird to distant star,
from star to love; and love grows
in the quiet house, turning and working,
servant of thought, a lamp held in one hand.

from Airs (1967)

from Airs (1967)

Fin d'hiver

Peu de chose, rien qui chasse
l'effroi de perdre l'espace
est laissé à l'âme errante

Mais peut-être, plus légère,
incertaine qu'elle dure,
est-elle celle qui chante
avec la voix la plus pure
les distances de la terre

End of Winter

Not much, nothing to dispel
the fear of wasting space
is left the itinerant soul

Except perhaps a voice
unconfident and light,
uncertainly put forth,
with which to celebrate
the reaches of the earth

Une semaison de larmes
sur le visage changé,
la scintillante saison
des rivières dérangées:
chagrin qui creuse la terre

L'âge regarde la neige
s'éloigner sur les montagnes

A dispersion of tears
on the changed face,
the glittering season
of rivers in spate,
grief scoring the earth

Age watches snow recede
from the mountain peaks

Dans l'herbe à l'hiver survivant
ces ombres moins pesantes qu'elle,
des timides bois patients
sont la discrète, la fidèle,

l'encore imperceptible mort

Toujours dans le jour tournant
ce vol autour de nos corps
Toujours dans le champ du jour
ces tombes d'ardoise bleue

These wood-shadows, timid, patient,
lighter even than the grass
that survived the winter,
are the discreet, faithful,

barely perceptible shadows of death

Always in the daytime
circling our bodies
Always in the open field
these tombstones of blue slate

Lune à l'aube d'été

Dans l'air de plus en plus clair
scintille encore cette larme
ou faible flamme dans du verre
quand du sommeil des montagnes
monte une vapeur dorée

Demeure ainsi suspendue
sur la balance de l'aube
entre la braise promise
et cette perle perdue

Dawn Moon

Through ever clearer air
there gleams still this tear,
a windowed candle–flame,
when from the sleep of mountains
rises a golden steam

Retain your balance there
in the summer dawn,
half promised ember,
half disregarded pearl

Lune d'hiver

Pour entrer dans l'obscurité
prends ce miroir où s'éteint
un glacial incendie:

atteint le centre de la nuit,
tu n'y verras plus reflété
qu'un baptême de brebis

Winter Moon

Before going out in the dark
take this mirror where
an icy blaze died:

once at the heart of night
you will find it reflects only
a baptism of sheep

Dans l'enceinte du bois d'hiver
sans entrer tu peux t'emparer
de l'unique lumière due:
elle n'est pas ardent bûcher
ni lampe aux branches suspendue

Elle est le jour sur l'écorce
l'amour qui se dissémine
peut-être la clarté divine
à qui la hache donne force

Without entering you can seize
the unique light locked
in the winter woods:
no bonfire this,
no lamp hung in the branches

But daybreak on the bark,
the love that fertilizes,
perhaps the holy light
an axe–flash emphasizes

Toute fleur n'est que de la nuit
qui feint de s'être rapprochée

Mais là d'où son parfum s'élève
je ne puis espérer entrer
c'est pourquoi tant il me trouble
et me fait si longtemps veiller
devant cette porte fermée

Toute couleur, toute vie
naît d'où le regard s'arrête

Ce monde n'est que la crête
d'un invisible incendie

Each flower is a little night
pretending to draw near

But where its scent rises
I cannot hope to enter
which is why it bothers me
so much and why I sit so long
before this closed door

Each colour, each incarnation
begins where the eyes stop

This world is merely the tip
of an unseen conflagration

Je marche
dans un jardin de braises fraîches
sous leur abri de feuilles

un charbon ardent sur la bouche

I walk in a garden
of ashes fresh
in their shelter of leaves

a burning coal on my lips

Tout à la fin de la nuit
quand ce souffle s'est élevé
une bougie d'abord
a défailli

Avant les premiers oiseaux
qui peut encore veiller?
Le vent le sait, qui traverse les fleuves

Cette flamme, ou larme inversée:
une obole pour le passeur

Right at the end of night
the wind rises
and the candle goes out

Who is there to keep watch
before the first birds?
The river-cold wind knows

A flame, an inverted tear:
a coin for the ferryman

Ah! l'idylle encore une fois
qui remonte du fond des prés
avec ses bergers naïfs

pour rien qu'une coupe embuée
où la bouche ne peut pas boire
pour rien qu'une grappe fraîche
brillant plus haut que Vénus!

The idyll once again
ascending from a field
of simple shepherds

for nothing but a cloudy cup
mouth cannot drink
for nothing but a cold grape
shining higher than Venus!

Martinets

Au moment orageux du jour
au moment hagard de la vie
ces faucilles au ras de la paille

Tout crie soudain plus haut
que ne peut gravir l'ouïe

Swifts

**At the stormy moment of dawn
at the apprehensive time
these sickles in the corn**

**Everything suddenly cries higher
than any ear can climb**

Fruits avec le temps plus bleus
comme endormis sous un masque de songe
dans la paille enflammée
et la poussière d'arrière-été

Nuit miroitante

Moment où l'on dirait
que la source même prend feu

Fruit bluer with time
dreaming asleep as if in thought
in the blazing straw
and late-summer dust

Glimmering night

A moment when the very
source seems to catch fire

Dans l'étendue
plus rien que des montagnes miroitantes

Plus rien que d'ardents regards
qui se croisent

Merles et ramiers

In the distance
nothing but shimmering peaks

Nothing but ardent glances
interweaving

Blackbirds and doves

Il y aura toujours dans mon oeil cependant
une invisible rose de regret
comme quand au-dessus d'un lac
a passé l'ombre d'un oiseau

Meanwhile my eye will retain
an invisible rose of regret
as when a bird-shadow
passes over a lake

Poids de pierres, des pensées

Songes et montagnes
n'ont pas même balance

Nous habitons encore un autre monde
peut-être l'intervalle

Weight of stones, of thoughts

Uneven balance
of mountain and dream

We still live in another world
perhaps the interval

Monde né d'une déchirure
apparu pour être fumée!

Néanmoins la lampe allumée
sur l'interminable lecture

World born of a lesion
and destined to be smoke!

Even so the lamplight
on an unfinishable book

from Leçons (1969)

from Lessons (1969)

Autrefois,
moi l'effrayé, l'ignorant, vivant à peine,
me couvrant d'images les yeux,
j'ai prétendu guider mourants et morts.

Moi, poète abrité,
épargné, souffrant à peine,
aller tracer des routes jusque-là!

À présent, lampe soufflée,
main plus errante, qui tremble,
je recommence lentement dans l'air.

Afraid, ignorant, scarcely alive,
I shielded my eyes with images once,
presuming to guide the dead and the dying.

Me, a sheltered poet,
reprieved, hardly suffering,
to go staking out tracks down there!

Now, my lamp extinguished,
my hand more shaky, wandering,
I slowly start again in the open air.

Raisins et figues
couvés au loin par les montagnes
sous les lents nuages
et la fraîcheur:
sans doute, sans doute . . .

Vient un moment où l'aîné se couche
presque sans force. On voit
de jour en jour
son pas moins assuré.

Il ne s'agit plus de passer
comme l'eau entre les herbes:
cela ne se tourne pas.

Lorsque le maître lui-même
si vite est emmené si loin,
je cherche ce qui peut le suivre:

ni la lanterne des fruits,
ni l'oiseau aventureux,
ni la plus pure des images;

plutôt le linge et l'eau changés,
la main qui veille,
plutôt le coeur endurant.

Grapes and figs
born far off in the mountains
under the slow clouds
and the fresh air –
oh yes, oh yes . . .

But there comes a time
when the eldest, tired,
retires early; from day to day
his step grows less assured.

No longer a question
of moving about
like water between its banks;
and this won't improve.

When the master himself
is taken so far so quickly
I look for what may follow –

not a lamp of fruit,
a fearless bird,
the purest of images,

but water and clean linen,
the loving hand
and the obstinate heart.

Je ne voudrais plus qu'éloigner
ce qui nous sépare du clair,
laisser seulement la place
à la bonté dédaignée.

J'écoute des hommes vieux
qui se sont accordés aux jours,
j'apprends à leurs pieds la patience:

ils n'ont pas de pire écolier.

I want only to remove
whatever blocks the light,
only to clear a space
for the despised gentleness.

I listen to old men,
their unanimous murmur,
and study patience at their feet.

They have no worse beginner.

Une stupeur
commençait dans ses yeux: que cela fût
possible. Une tristesse aussi,
vaste comme ce qui venait sur lui,
qui brisait les barrières de sa vie,
vertes, pleines d'oiseaux.

Lui qui avait toujours aimé son clos, ses murs,
lui qui gardait les clefs de la maison.

A stupor started in his eyes
that such a thing should be possible;
sadness too, as vast
as the darkness coming upon him, crashing
the leaved-with-birdsong
gates of his life.

He who had always loved his garden, his walls,
who had kept the keys of the house.

Entre la plus lointaine étoile et nous,
la distance, inimaginable, reste encore
comme une ligne, un lien, comme un chemin.
S'il est un lieu hors de toute distance,
ce devait être là qu'il se perdait:
non pas plus loin de toute étoile, ni moins loin,
mais déjà presque dans un autre espace,
en dehors, entraîné hors des mesures.
Notre mètre, de lui à nous, n'avait plus cours:
autant, comme une lame, le briser sur le genou.

Between us and the farthest star
lie the unthinkable distances –
lines, tracks, paths. If there
is a place beyond this space
it would be there he disappeared:
neither farther nor less far
but in another space, abstracted
beyond measure. The ruler laid
from us to him lost continuity
like a sword broken across the knee.

'Qui m'aidera? Nul ne peut venir jusqu'ici.
Qui me tiendrait les mains ne tiendrait pas celles qui tremblent,
qui mettrait un écran devant mes yeux ne me garderait pas de voir,
qui serait jour et nuit autour de moi comme un manteau
ne pourrait rien contre ce feu, contre ce froid.
D'ici, j'atteste au moins qu'il est un mur
qu'aucun engin, qu'aucune trompette n'ébranle.
Rien ne m'attend plus désormais que le plus long et le pire.'

Est-ce ainsi qu'il se tait dans l'étroitesse de la nuit?

'Who will help me? No one can come this far.
Holding my hands won't stop them shaking,
shading my eyes won't stop them seeing,
being close to me day and night like a coat
can do nothing against this heat, this cold.
I can at least confirm there is a wall here
that no invading force will ever destroy.
There's nothing for it now but the longest and worst.'

Is this what he whispers to the narrowing night?

C'est sur nous maintenant
comme une montagne en surplomb.

Dans son ombre glacée,
on est réduit à vénérer et à vomir.

À peine ose-t-on voir.

Quelque chose s'enfonce pour détruire.
Quelle pitié
quand l'autre monde enfonce dans un corps
son coin!

N'attendez pas
que je marie la lumière à ce fer.

Le front contre le mur de la montagne
dans le jour froid,
nous sommes pleins d'horreur et de pitié.

Dans le jour hérissé d'oiseaux.

It's over us now
like a mountainous shadow.

An icy shadow in which
we can only pray and vomit.

It's hard to watch.

Something buries itself in him to kill.
The pity of it
when the other world sinks its blade
in a living body!

Don't ask me
to forge light from this iron.

Our heads against the mountain
in the cold dawn,
we are filled with horror and pity.

In the dawn bristling with birds.

On peut nommer cela horreur, ordure,
prononcer même les mots de l'ordure
déchiffrés dans le linge des bas-fonds:
à quelque singerie que se livre le poète,
cela n'entrera pas dans sa page d'écriture.

Ordure non à dire ni à voir:
à dévorer.

En même temps,
simple comme de la terre.

Se peut-il que la plus épaisse nuit
n'enveloppe cela?

L'illimité accouple ou déchire.

On sent un remugle de vieux dieux.

The horror, the shit –
go on, describe the shit
inscribed on the bed linen.
Whatever the poet's fancy flights
they won't get on to the printed page.

Shit not to name or to see
but to devour.

At the same time
as simple as earth.

And maybe the thickest night
won't cover it up.

The limitless joins or dissevers.

A stink of ancient gods.

Misère
comme une montagne sur nous écroulée.

Pour avoir fait pareille déchirure,
ce ne peut être un rêve simplement qui se dissipe.

L'homme, s'il n'était qu'un noeud d'air,
faudrait-il, pour le dénouer, fer si tranchant?

Bourrés de larmes, tous, le front contre ce mur,
plutôt que son inconsistance,
n'est-ce pas la réalité de notre vie
qu'on nous apprend?

Instruits au fouet.

Misery
like a mountain burying us.

To have torn so much
it can't be merely a waking dream.

If man were only a knot of air
would he need so sharp an edge to untie it?

Bursting with tears, our heads against the wall,
are we not rather learning
the reality of life
than its insubstantiality?

Instructed by the whip.

Plus aucun souffle.

Comme quand le vent du matin
a eu raison
de la dernière bougie.

Il y a en nous un si profond silence
qu'une comète
en route vers la nuit des filles de nos filles,
nous l'entendrions.

No breathing now.

As when the dawn wind
has done its worst
with the last candle.

So great is the silence among us
we could hear a comet
on its way to the night
of our daughters' daughters.

S'il se pouvait (qui saura jamais rien?)
qu'il ait encore un espèce d'être aujourd'hui,
de conscience même que l'on croirait proche,
serait-ce donc ici qu'il se tiendrait,
dans cet enclos, non pas dans la prairie?
Se pourrait-il qu'il attendît ici
comme à un rendez-vous donné 'près de la pierre',
qu'il eut l'emploi de nos pas muets, de nos larmes?
Comment savoir? Un jour ou l'autre, on voit
ces pierres s'enfoncer dans les herbes éternelles,
tôt ou tard il n'y a plus d'hôtes à convier
au repère à son tour enfoui,
plus même d'ombres dans nulle ombre.

If it should be, and who can ever be sure,
that he still has some kind of existence today,
of consciousness even, not too far away,
would it be here that he would stay,
in the garden rather than out in the pasture?
Might he be waiting there, as if
by arrangement, 'beside the stone'?
Might he have need of our voices, our tears?
I don't know; but one day or another will see
these stones buried by the eternal grass,
sooner or later there will be no one left
to visit the grave, which will be buried too,
not even shadows in that shadowless place.

Toi cependant,

ou tout à fait effacé
et nous laissant moins de cendres
que feu d'un soir au foyer,

ou invisible habitant l'invisible,

ou graine dans la loge de nos coeurs,

quoi qu'il en soit,

demeure en modèle de patience et de sourire,
tel le soleil dans notre dos encore
qui éclaire la table, et la page, et les raisins.

You meanwhile,

whether altogether in shadow
and leaving us fewer ashes
than a grate at night,

whether invisible with the invisible

or a seed lodged in our hearts,

whatever you are,

you remain our example
of smiling fortitude
like the sun at our backs illuminating
the table, the page and the grapes.

from Chants d'en bas (1974)

from Songs from Below (1974)

Parler est facile, et tracer des mots sur la page,
en règle générale, est risquer peu de chose:
un ouvrage de dentellière, calfeutré,
paisible (on a pu même demander
à la bougie une clarté plus douce, plus trómpeuse),
tous les mots sont écrits de la même encre,
'fleur' et 'peur' par exemple sont presque pareils,
et j'aurai beau répéter 'sang' de haut en bas
de la page, elle n'en sera pas tachée,
ni moi blessé.

Aussi arrive-t-il qu'on prenne ce jeu en horreur,
qu'on ne comprenne plus ce qu'on a voulu faire
en y jouant, au lieu de se risquer dehors
et de faire meilleur usage de ses mains.

Cela,
c'est quand on ne peut plus se dérober à la douleur,
qu'elle ressemble à quelqu'un qui approche
en déchirant les brumes dont on s'enveloppe,
abattant un à un les obstacles, traversant
la distance de plus en plus faible – si près soudain
qu'on ne voit plus que son mufle plus large
que le ciel.

Parler alors semble mensonge, ou pire: lâche
insulte à la douleur, et gaspillage
du peu de temps et de forces qui nous reste.

It's easy to talk, and writing words on the page
doesn't involve much risk as a general rule:
you might as well be knitting late at night
in a warm room, in a soft, treacherous light.
The words are all written in the same ink,
'flower' and 'fear' are nearly the same for example,
and I could scrawl 'blood' the length of the page
without splashing the paper or hurting
myself at all.

After a while it gets you down, this game,
you no longer know what it was you set out to achieve
instead of exposing yourself to life
and doing something useful with your hands.

That's when you can't escape,
when pain is a figure tearing the fog
that shrouds you, striking away
the obstacles one by one, covering
the swiftly decreasing distance, now
so close you can make out nothing
but his mug wider than the sky.

To speak is to lie, or worse: a craven
insult to grief or a waste
of the little time and energy at our disposal.

Y aurait-il des choses qui habitent les mots
plus volontiers, et qui s'accordent avec eux
– ces moments de bonheur qu'on retrouve dans les poèmes
avec bonheur, une lumière qui franchit les mots
comme en les effaçant – et d'autres choses
qui se cabrent contre eux, les altèrent, qui les détruisent:

comme si la parole rejetait la mort,
ou plutôt, que la mort fît pourrir
même les mots?

Might there be things which lend themselves
more readily to words, and live with them
– those glad moments gladly found in poems,
light that releases words
as if erasing them; while other things
resist them, change them, destroy them even –

as if language resisted death,
or rather, as if death consumed
even the words?

Déchire ces ombres enfin comme chiffons,
vêtu de loques, faux mendiant, coureur de linceuls:
singer la mort à distance est vergogne,
avoir peur quand il y aura lieu suffit. À présent,
habille-toi d'une fourrure de soleil et sors
comme un chasseur contre le vent, franchis
comme une eau fraîche et rapide ta vie.

Si tu avais moins peur,
tu ne ferais plus d'ombre sur tes pas.

Tear these shadows like rags,
tramp, pseudo-mendicant, shroud-chaser.
The shame of aping death at a distance,
of showing fear before the event . . .
Wrap yourself in a cape of sunlight,
step like a hunter into the wind,
quicken your life like spring-water.

Were you less afraid,
you would cast no shadow before you.

Écris vite ce livre, achève vite aujourd'hui ce poème
avant que le doute de toi ne te rattrape,
la nuée des questions qui t'égare et te fait broncher,
ou pire que cela . . .
                    Cours au bout de la ligne,
comble ta page avant que ne fasse trembler
tes mains la peur – de t'égarer, d'avoir mal, d'avoir peur,
avant que l'air ne cède à quoi tu es adossé
pour quelque temps encore, le beau mur bleu.
Parfois déjà la cloche se dérègle dans le beffroi d'os
et boite à en fendre les murs.

Écris, non pas 'à l'ange de l'église de Laodicée',
mais sans savoir à qui, dans l'air, avec des signes
hésitants, inquiets, de chauve-souris,
vite, franchis encore cette distance avec ta main,
relie, tisse en hâte, encore, habille-nous,
bêtes frileuses, nous taupes maladroites,
couvre-nous d'un dernier pan doré de jour
comme le soleil fait aux peupliers et aux montagnes.

Quick write this book, quick finish this poem today
before self-doubt can hinder you,
before the distracting cloud
of questions leads you astray.

Finish the line, fill up the page before
the trembling starts, the trembling born
of illness, fear, distraction,
before thin air replaces the blue wall
you're leaning against. Sometimes already
the bell goes wrong in the bone belfry,
banging fit to split the stones.

Don't write 'for the angel in the church of the Laodiceans'
but without knowing for whom, on the air,
with uncertain, tentative bat-signs.
Quick, clear this space again with your hand;
bind, weave, clothe us shivering beasts,
us baffled moles, cover us up
with a last strip of golden light
as the sun covers the poplars and the mountains.

Je me redresse avec effort et je regarde:
il y a trois lumières, dirait-on.
Celle du ciel, celle qui de là-haut
s'écoule en moi, s'efface,
et celle dont ma main trace l'ombre sur la page.

L'encre serait de l'ombre.

Le ciel qui me traverse me surprend.

On voudrait croire que nous sommes tourmentés
pour mieux monter le ciel. Mais le tourment
l'emporte sur ces envolées, et la pitié
noie tout, brillant d'autant de larmes
que la nuit.

I rise with an effort and look out
at three different kinds of light –
that of the sky, that which from up there
pours into me and vanishes,
and that whose shadow my hand draws on the page.

The ink might be mistaken for shadow.

The sky descending takes me by surprise.

One would like to believe we suffer
to describe the light from above;
but pain is stronger than flight
and pity drowns everything, shining
with as many tears as the night.

from À la lumière d'hiver (1977)

from Winter Light (1977)

Fleurs, oiseaux, fruits, c'est vrai, je les ai conviés,
je les ai vus, montrés, j'ai dit:
'c'est la fragilité même qui est la force',
facile à dire! et trop facile de jongler
avec le poids des choses une fois changées en mots!
On bâtissait le char d'Élie avec des graines
légères, des souffles, des lueurs, on prétendait
se vêtir d'air comme les oiseaux et les saints . . .

Frêles signes, maison de brume ou d'étincelles,
jeunesse . . .
                    puis les portes se ferment en grinçant
l'une après l'autre.

Et néanmoins je dis encore,
non plus porté par la course du sang, non plus ailé,
hors de tout enchantement,
trahi par tous les magiciens et tous les dieux,
depuis longtemps fui par les nymphes
même au bord des rivières transparentes
et même à l'aube,
                        mais en me forçant à parler, plus têtu
que l'enfant quand il grave avec peine son nom
sur la table d'école,

j'insiste, quoique je ne sache plus les mots,
quoique ce ne soit pas ainsi la juste voie
– qui est droite comme la course de l'amour
vers la cible, la rose le soir enflammée,
alors que moi, j'ai une canne obscure
qui, plus qu'elle ne trace aucun chemin, ravage
la dernière herbe sur ses bords, semée
peut-être un jour par la lumière pour un plus
hardi marcheur . . .

Flowers, birds, fruit, I've gathered them all,
studied them, explained them, saying,
'Their strength lies in their very delicacy' –
easy to say, and easy too to play
with weighty matters when transformed to words.
I made my Elijah's chariot
of pollen, breath, velleities,
that it might take to the air like a bird or a saint.

Dim signs, home of mist and sparks,
youth . . .
             then, creaking, the doors close
one by one.

             Yet I go on talking,
a thin trickle now, no wings,
expelled from trance,
abandoned by the wondrous gods,
long since deserted by the nymphs
even at the edge of the clearest river,
even at daybreak,
                 forcing myself to speak,
absorbed like a child painstakingly
carving his name on a school desk.

I go on, even though I've forgotten the words,
even though this isn't the right direction –
which is as straight as the flight of love
to its target, the blazing rose at dusk
where my dark walking-stick
traces no path but levels
a last flower at the roadside
sown one day by the light perhaps
for a bolder pilgrim . . .

'Oui, oui, c'est vrai, j'ai vu la mort au travail
et, sans aller chercher la mort, le temps aussi,
tout près de moi, sur moi, j'en donne acte à mes deux yeux,
adjudgé! Sur la douleur, on en aurait trop long à dire.
Mais quelque chose n'est pas entamé par ce couteau
ou se referme après son coup comme l'eau derrière la barque.'

'It's true, of course, that I've seen death at work
and, not to speak of death, time too –
beside me, in me, in my failing eyes.
Regarding pain, words are inadequate;
but something remains unharmed by the knife
whose incision closes like water behind a ship.'

(Chose brève, le temps de quelques pas dehors,
mais plus étrange encore que les mages et les dieux.)

(Nothing at all, a footfall on the road,
yet more mysterious than guide or god.)

Nuages de novembre, oiseaux sombres par bandes qui traînez
et laissez après vous aux montagnes un peu
des plumes blanches de vos ventres,
longs miroirs des routes désertes, des fossés,
terre de plus en plus visible et grande, tombe
et déjà berceau des herbes,
                                        le secret qui vous lie,
arrive-t-il qu'on cesse de l'entendre un jour?

Écoute, écoute mieux, derrière
tous les murs, à travers le vacarme croissant
qui est en toi et hors de toi,
écoute . . . Et puise dans l'eau invisible
où peut-être boivent encore d'invisibles bêtes
après d'autres, depuis toujours, qui sont venues,
silencieuses, blanches, lentes, ou couchant
(ayant été dès l'aube obéissantes au soleil sur le grand pré),
laper cette lumière qui ne s'éteint pas la nuit
mais seulement se couvre d'ombre, à peine,
comme se couvrent les troupeaux d'un manteau de sommeil.

November clouds, dark flights of trailing birds
leaving behind you on the mountain bits
of your white down, reflecting
empty roads and ditches,
earth rising to meet you,
a grave where young grass grows,
will your mystery be lost at the end of the day?

Listen harder, ignore the noise
inside and out. Drink the invisible
pool where invisible creatures drink
as their ancestors have drunk since time began
at sunset, silent, white and slow,
having watched since dawn the sun in the meadow . . .
Absorb this light no night extinguishes
but only, barely, wraps itself in shadow
as flocks wrap themselves in a blanket of sleep.

. . . Et le ciel serait-il clément tout un hiver,
le laboureur avec patience ayant conduit ce soc
où peut-être Vénus aura paru parfois
entre la boue et les buées de l'aube,
verra-t-il croître en mars, à ras de terre,
une herbe autre que l'herbe?

. . . And if the heavens were mild a winter long,
the patient ploughman having drawn
his blade where, in the mud and mist
of dawn, the light of Venus shone,
would March notice, stubbling the face
of earth, grass which was more than grass?

Les larmes quelquefois montent aux yeux
comme d'une source,
elles sont de la brume sur des lacs,
un trouble du jour intérieur,
une eau que la peine a salée.

Le seule grâce à demander aux dieux lointains,
aux dieux muets, aveugles, détournés,
à ces fuyards,
ne serait-elle pas que toute larme répandue
sur le visage proche
dans l'invisible terre fit germer
un blé inépuisable?

Our eyes fill with tears sometimes
as if with spring-water:
these are lake mists,
clouds in our mental sky,
water sharp with the salt of pain.

The one favour we can ask of the distant gods,
the dumb, blind renegades,
deserters,
might it not be that every tear
on a familiar face
sow the invisible earth
with inexhaustible wheat?

L'hiver, le soir: alors, parfois, l'espace
ressemble à une chambre boisée
avec des rideaux bleus de plus en plus sombres
où s'usent les derniers reflets du feu,
puis la neige s'allume contre le mur
telle une lampe froide.

Où serait-ce déjà la lune qui, en s'élevant,
se lave de toute poussière
et de la buée de nos bouches?

A winter evening . . . Sometimes space
seems like a panelled room,
blue curtains darkening,
the fire flickering out
while a cold lamp
of snow shines against the wall.

Or is it the moon already rising
cleansed of her dust
and the breath of our mouths?

Sur tout cela maintenant je voudrais
que descende la neige, lentement,
qu'elle se pose sur les choses tout au long du jour
– elle qui parle toujours à voix basse –
et qu'elle fasse le sommeil des graines,
d'être ainsi protégé, plus patient.

Et nous saurions que le soleil encore,
cependant, passe au-delà,
que, si elle se lasse, il redeviendra même un moment
visible, comme la bougie derrière son écran jauni.

Alors, je me ressouviendrais de ce visage
qui demeure, lui aussi, derrière
la lente chute des cristaux humides,
qui change, avec ses yeux limpides ou en larmes,
impatiemment fidèles . . .
                     Et, caché par la neige,
de nouveau j'oserais louer leur clarté bleu.

On all of which I would like snow
to fall now, softly;
to drift all day
with its quiet continuous voice;
to fill with patience
the seeds asleep in its care.

Meanwhile the sun
would still pass overhead
and, when the snow stopped, reappear
like a candle from behind its yellow screen.

And that would remind me of a face
which also hides behind
a slow drift of damp crystals;
which changes, the eyes clear or cloudy,
impatient and faithful . . .
                    Hidden by snow,
I would dare praise their blue light once again.

Fidèles yeux de plus en plus faibles jusqu'à
ce que les miens se ferment, et après eux, l'espace
comme un éventail peint dont il ne resterait plus
qu'une frêle manche d'os, une trace glacée
pour les seuls yeux sans paupières d'autres astres.

Such faithful eyes weaker and weaker until
my own eyes close; then space itself
like a painted fan of which nothing remains
but a frail stick of bone, an icy trace
for the lidless eyes of other stars alone.

from Pensées sous les nuages (1983)

from Cloud Thoughts (1983)

On voit

On voit les écoliers courir à grands cris
dans l'herbe épaisse du préau.

Les hauts arbres tranquilles
et la lumière de dix heures en septembre
comme une fraîche cascade
les abritent encore de l'énorme enclume
qui étincelle d'étoiles par-delà.

★

L'âme, si frileuse, si farouche,
devra-t-elle vraiment marcher sans fin sur ce glacier,
seule, pieds nus, ne sachant plus même épeler
sa prière d'enfance,
sans fin punie de sa froideur par ce froid?

★

Elle s'approche du miroir rond
comme une bouche d'enfant
qui ne sait pas mentir,
vêtue d'une robe de chambre bleue
qui s'use elle aussi.

Cheveux bientôt couleur de cendre
sous le très lent feu du temps.

Le soleil du petit matin
fortifie encore son ombre.

★

Derrière la fenêtre dont on a blanchi le cadre
(contre les mouches, contre les fantômes),
une tête chenue de vieil homme se penche
sur une lettre, ou les nouvelles du pays.
Le lierre sombre croît contre le mur.

Gardez-le, lierre et chaux, du vent de l'aube,
des nuits trop longues et de l'autre, éternelle.

Glimpses

The children run shouting
in the thick grass of the playground.

The tall tranquil trees
and the torrential light
of a September morning
protect them still from the anvil
sparkling with stars up there.

★

The soul, so chilly, so fierce, must it really
trudge up this glacier for ever,
solitary, in bare feet, no longer
remembering even its childhood prayer,
its coldness for ever punished by this cold?

★

Wrapped in a blue bath-robe
which is wearing out too,
she goes to a mirror round
like the mouth of a child
who doesn't know how to lie.

Hair the colour of ash now
in the slow burn of time;

and yet the morning sun
quickens her shadow still.

★

At the window with its freshly whitewashed frame
(to keep out flies, to keep out ghosts)
the white head of an old man leans
over a letter or the local news.
Against the wall dark ivy grows.

Save him, ivy and lime, from the dawn wind,
from long nights and the other, eternal night.

Le mot joie

Je suis comme quelqu'un qui creuse dans la brume
à la recherche de ce qui échappe à la brume
pour avoir entendu un peu plus loin des pas
et des paroles entre des passants échangées . . .
★
L'aurais-je donc inventé, le pinceau du couchant
sur la toile rugueuse de la terre,
l'huile dorée du soir sur les prairies et sur les bois?

C'était pourtant comme la lampe sur la table avec le pain.
★
Mais chaque jour, peut-être, on peut reprendre
le filet déchiré, maille après maille,
et ce serait, dans l'espace plus haut,
comme recoudre, astre à astre, la nuit . . .
★
Comme on voit maintenant dans les jardins de février
brûler ces petits feux de feuilles
(et l'on dirait que c'est moins pour nettoyer
le clos que pour aider la lumière à s'élargir),
est-il bien vrai que nous ne pouvons plus
en faire autant, avec notre coeur invisible?
★
Qu'on me le montre, celui qui aurait conquis la certitude
et qui rayonnerait à partir de là dans la paix
comme une montagne qui s'éteint la dernière
et ne frémit jamais sous la pesée de la nuit.

The Word Joy

I am searching here in the fog
for something escaped from the fog
having heard steps in the distance
and the voices of passers-by.

★

Perhaps I imagined it, the sunset brush
on the rough canvas of earth,
a golden evening oil
on fields and woods; but it looked
like the lamplight and the bread on a kitchen table.

★

Each day, perhaps, you might replace
the stitches in the severed net –
thus, in the distances of space,
to sew up, star by star, the night.

★

These bonfires in the February gardens
lit less for tidiness, you would say,
than to help spread the light,
can we ourselves manage no more
than this with our secret heart?

★

Show me the man who has found certitude
and shines in peace like the last
peak to fade at twilight, never
wincing under the weight of night.

À Henry Purcell

Écoute: comment se peut-il
que notre voix troublée se mêle ainsi
aux étoiles?

Il lui a fait gravir le ciel
sur des degrés de verre
par la grâce juvénile de son art.

★

Il nous a fait entendre le passage des brebis
qui se pressent dans la poussière de l'été céleste
et dont nous n'avons jamais bu le lait.

Il les a rassemblées dans la bergerie nocturne
où de la paille brille entre les pierres.
La barrière sonore est refermée:
fraîcheur de ces paisibles herbes à jamais.

★

Songe à ce que serait pour ton ouïe,
toi qui es à l'écoute de la nuit,
une très lente neige
de cristal.

★

On imagine une comète
qui reviendrait après des siècles
du royaume des morts
et, cette nuit, traverserait le nôtre
en y semant les mêmes graines . . .

★

Pendant que j'écoute,
le reflet d'une bougie
tremble dans le miroir
comme une flamme tressée
à de l'eau.

Cette voix aussi, n'est-elle pas l'écho
d'une autre, plus réelle?
Va-t-il l'entendre, celui qui se débat
entre les mains toujours trop lentes
du bourreau?
L'entendrai-je, moi?

Si jamais ils parlent au-dessus de nous
entre les arbres constellés de leur avril.

★

To Henry Purcell

Listen: how is it
that our troubled voice mingles like this
with the stars?

He has scaled the heavens
on rungs of glass
by the youthful grace of his art.

★

We hear the passing of ewes
who throng the dust of the celestial summer,
whose milk we have never drunk.

He has herded them into the fold of night
where straw shines among the stones,
and the gate bangs shut.
The coolness of these quiet grasses for ever . . .

★

What do we hear
who tune in to the night?
A leisurely snow
of crystal.

★

Imagine a comet
returning centuries hence
from the kingdom of the dead,
crossing our century tonight
and sowing the same seeds . . .

★

While I listen
the reflection of a candle
flickers in the mirror
like a flame woven
of water.

Might not this voice be the echo
of another, more real?
And will that ever be heard
by those thrashing in terror?
Will I hear it myself?

If ever they speak above us
in the starry trees of their April.

★

Tu es assis
devant le métier haut dressé de cette harpe.

Même invisible, je t'ai reconnu,
tisserand des ruisseaux surnaturels.

You are seated before
the tense loom of the harp.

I know you, though invisible,
weaver of supernatural streams.

Index